Written by Gerald Hacker & Andrew Wolthers
Illustrated by Ryan Adamson
Edited by Rachelle Burk & Sara Hays

Copyright © 2014
GameRules4Kids.com • Birmingham, AL

Published by **GAMERULES**

ISBN: 978-0-9882895-4-3

Created in the U.S.A. Printed in the USA. All rights reserved. No part of this publication may be reproduced, stored in a retrieval system or transmitted in any form or by any means electronic, mechanical, photocopied, recorded or otherwise, without the prior written permission of the copyright owner.

BASEBALL FIELD DIAGRAM

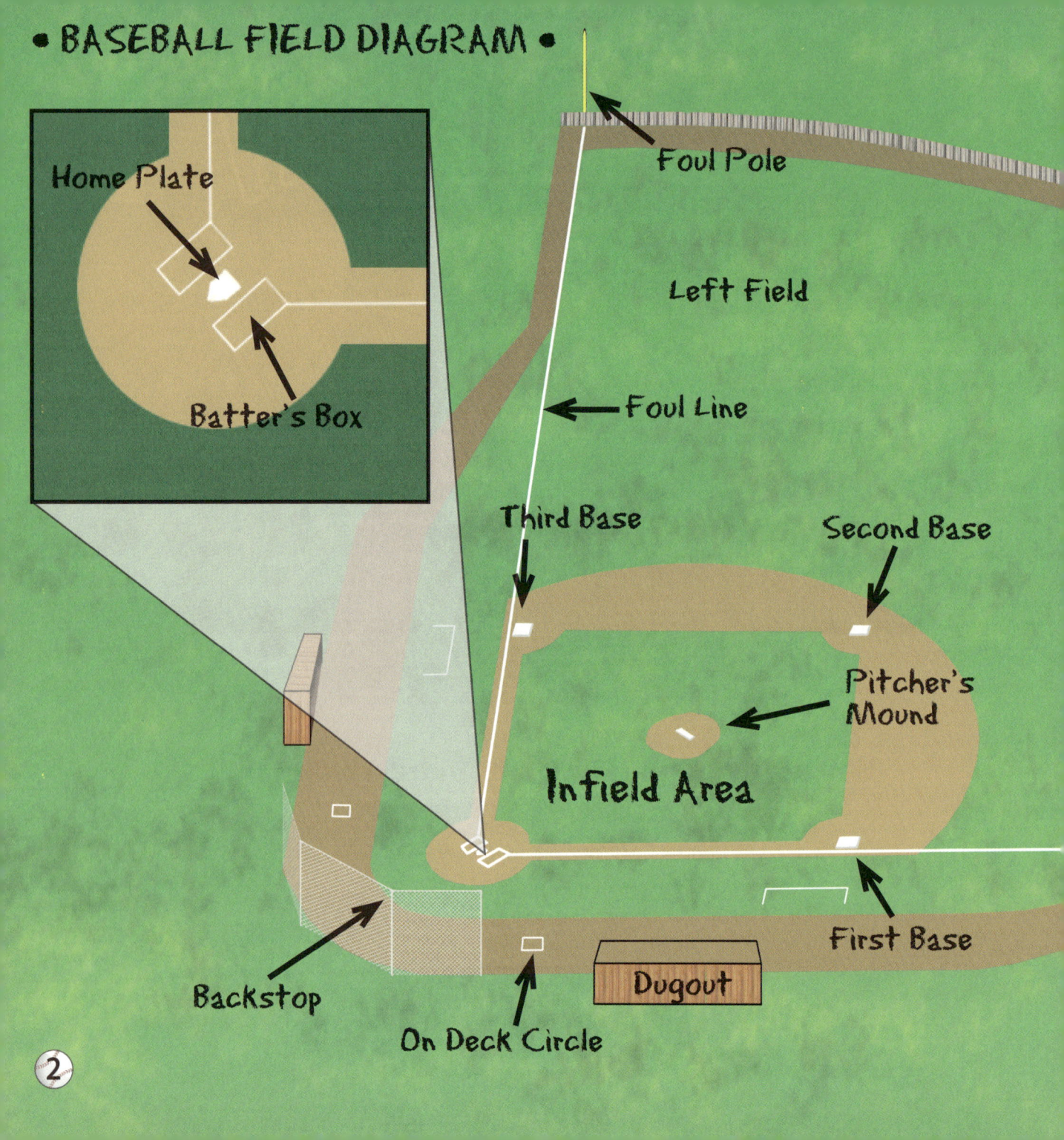

- Home Plate
- Batter's Box
- Foul Pole
- Left Field
- Foul Line
- Third Base
- Second Base
- Pitcher's Mound
- Infield Area
- First Base
- Backstop
- Dugout
- On Deck Circle

Outfield Fence

Outfield Area

Center Field

Right Field

Bullpen

TOPICS COVERED:

- Batting
- Pitching
- Balls / Strikes
- Strike Zone
- Walk
- Umpire
- Out
- Strikeout
- Positions
- Fly Out
- Tag Out
- Force Out
- Fly Ball
- Line Drive
- Ground Ball
- Batting Order
- Innings
- Home Team / Visiting Team
- Foul / Fair Ball
- Base Hit
- Single
- Double
- Triple
- Home Run
- Slide
- Run
- Scoring Position
- Base Coach
- Safe
- Error
- Tagging Up
- Sacrifice Fly
- Base Running
- Double Play
- Triple Play
- Check Swing
- Wild Pitch
- Signs
- Steal
- Hit and Run
- Pinch Hitter
- Sacrifice
- Bunt
- Cut-Off Man

The game was nearly over. The Knights were ahead by one. Brady stood in ready position.
If this ball is hit anywhere near me, I'm catching it, thought Brady.

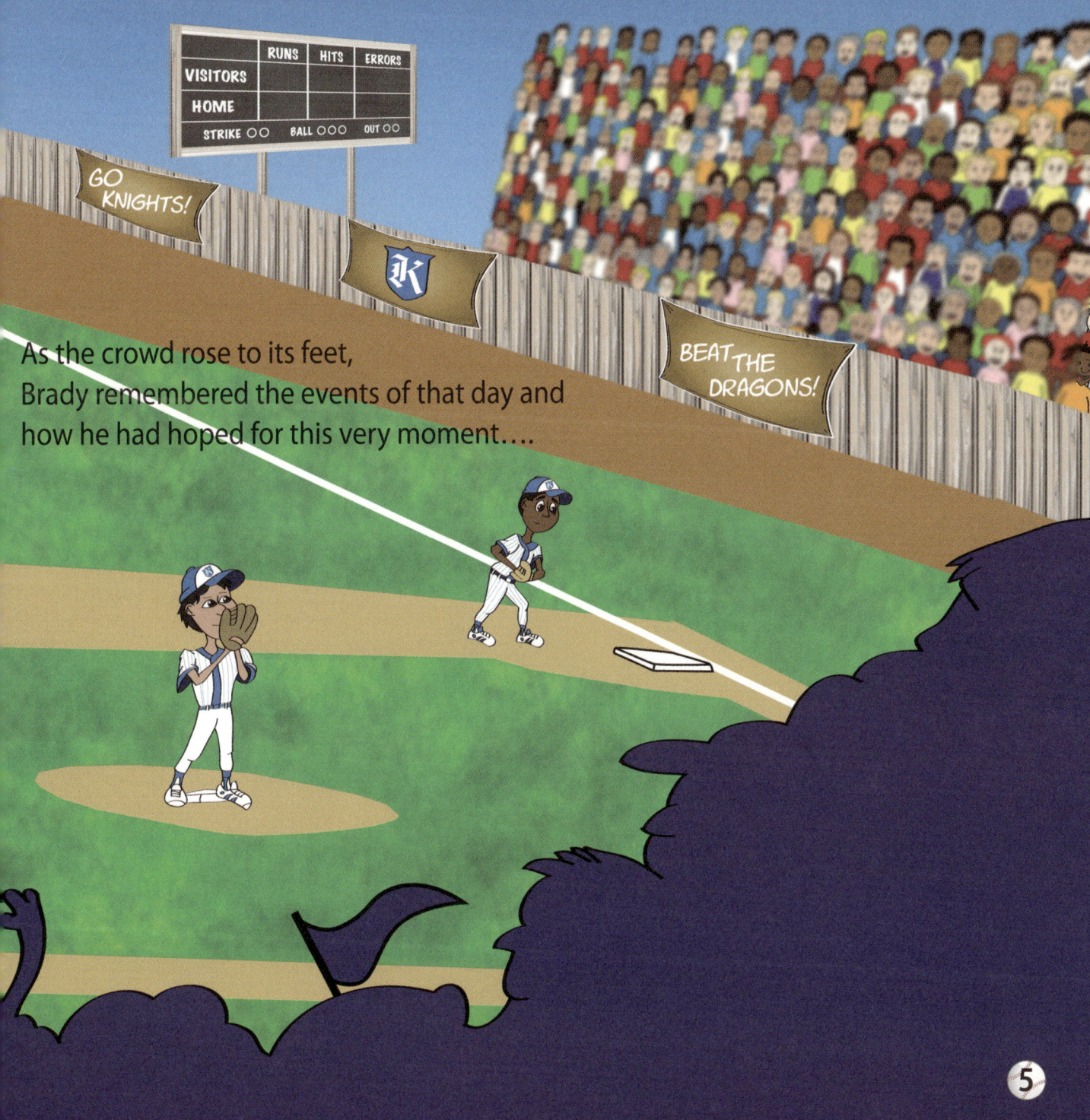

Brady's dad leaned down to help him. "As long as you remember the three most important things when you play, you'll do just fine," he said. **"Have a good attitude, give your best effort, and have fun!"** said Brady.

As the players arrived at the field, Coach Martin gathered the Knights for **batting** practice. Brady's friend Chris was **pitching** that night, so he started warming up outside the batting cage. While the players took turns inside the batting cage, Brady and his teammates acted like the **umpire** by calling **balls** and **strikes** on one another.

PITCHING and BATTING are the key parts in a baseball play. Pitching is done from the *pitcher's mound*, while the batter stands in the *batter's box* to hit. The pitch is called a BALL or a STRIKE by the UMPIRE depending on whether the pitch is in the *strike zone*, an area as wide as home plate between the batter's knees and chest. Three strikes against a batter count as a STRIKEOUT, while four balls count as a WALK and allow the batter to go to first base.

"You're **out**!" teased Brady when his buddy Anthony swung and missed from inside the cage. Anthony grinned back at him, thankful it wasn't a real **strikeout**.
"Keep in mind, a **walk** is just as good as hitting the ball to get on base," reminded Coach Martin.

An OUT is the goal of the *fielding* team on defense. The batting team gets three outs during its turn to bat. The pitcher can get an out by striking out the batter, but other outs happen once the batter hits the ball into play. Once a player is called out, he must return to the dugout.

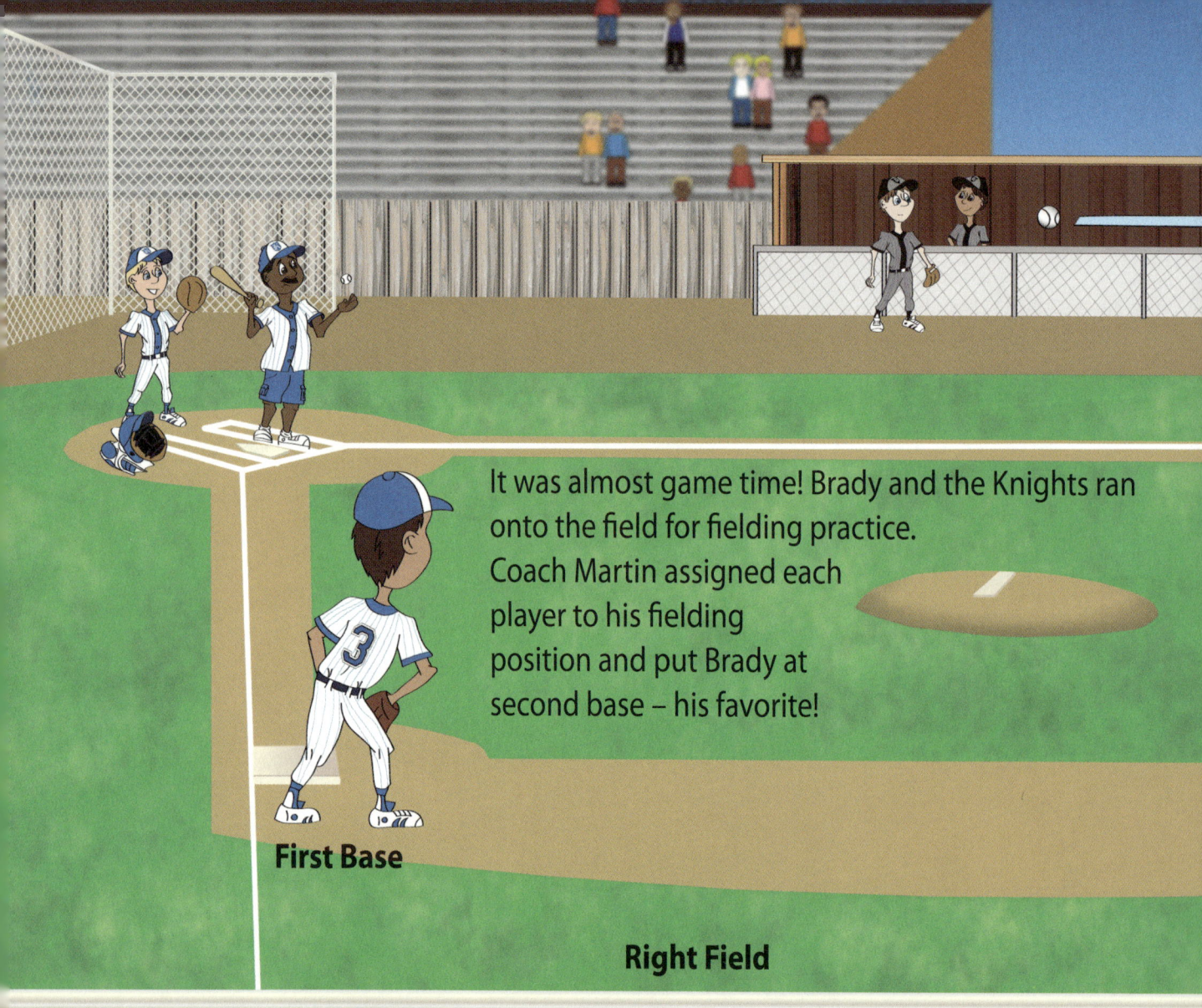

It was almost game time! Brady and the Knights ran onto the field for fielding practice. Coach Martin assigned each player to his fielding position and put Brady at second base – his favorite!

First Base

Right Field

A FLY BALL is one which is hit high in the air, while a LINE DRIVE is a hard hit ball which travels level to the ground. A FLY OUT is when either type of ball is caught before hitting the ground. A GROUND BALL is any batted ball that hits the ground before being caught by the defense.

The team warmed up by practicing each kind of fielding out: **fly outs**, **tag outs**, and **force outs**. Coach Martin hit **line drives** and **ground balls** to the infielders and **fly balls** to the outfielders.

A TAG OUT happens when a base runner is tagged by a fielding player before he can reach a base. A FORCE OUT happens on ground balls when the fielding player touches the base before a runner who is trying to reach that base. However, a force out can only happen if a base runner is being "forced" to run by another runner behind him. The batting player can always be "forced out" at first base, and a player starting at first base can always be forced out at second base.

The teams finished their warm-ups and went to their dugouts. Coach Martin announced the **batting order** while the team prepared for the 1st **inning**. Brady was batting third. "PLAY BALL!" bellowed the home plate umpire, and the game was underway.

The BATTING ORDER or lineup is the order in which each player on a team gets to take his turn batting. When the last player in the lineup has batted, the order starts over again with the first batter.

INNINGS are the way a baseball game is divided up. Each team gets three outs in every inning during its turn to bat.

The Knights were batting first as the **visiting team**. The Dragons were the **home team** and would have the last at bat. Brady watched as the first two batters both made outs in front of him.
"Just try to get on base," Coach Martin instructed.
Brady left the on-deck circle and walked toward home plate.

The VISITING TEAM bats first in an inning (called the *top* part of the inning), and the HOME TEAM bats last (called the *bottom* part of the inning). Games will usually last anywhere between five to nine innings with the home team always getting the last at bat if necessary. Extra innings can be played to determine the winner if teams are tied at the end of the regular game.

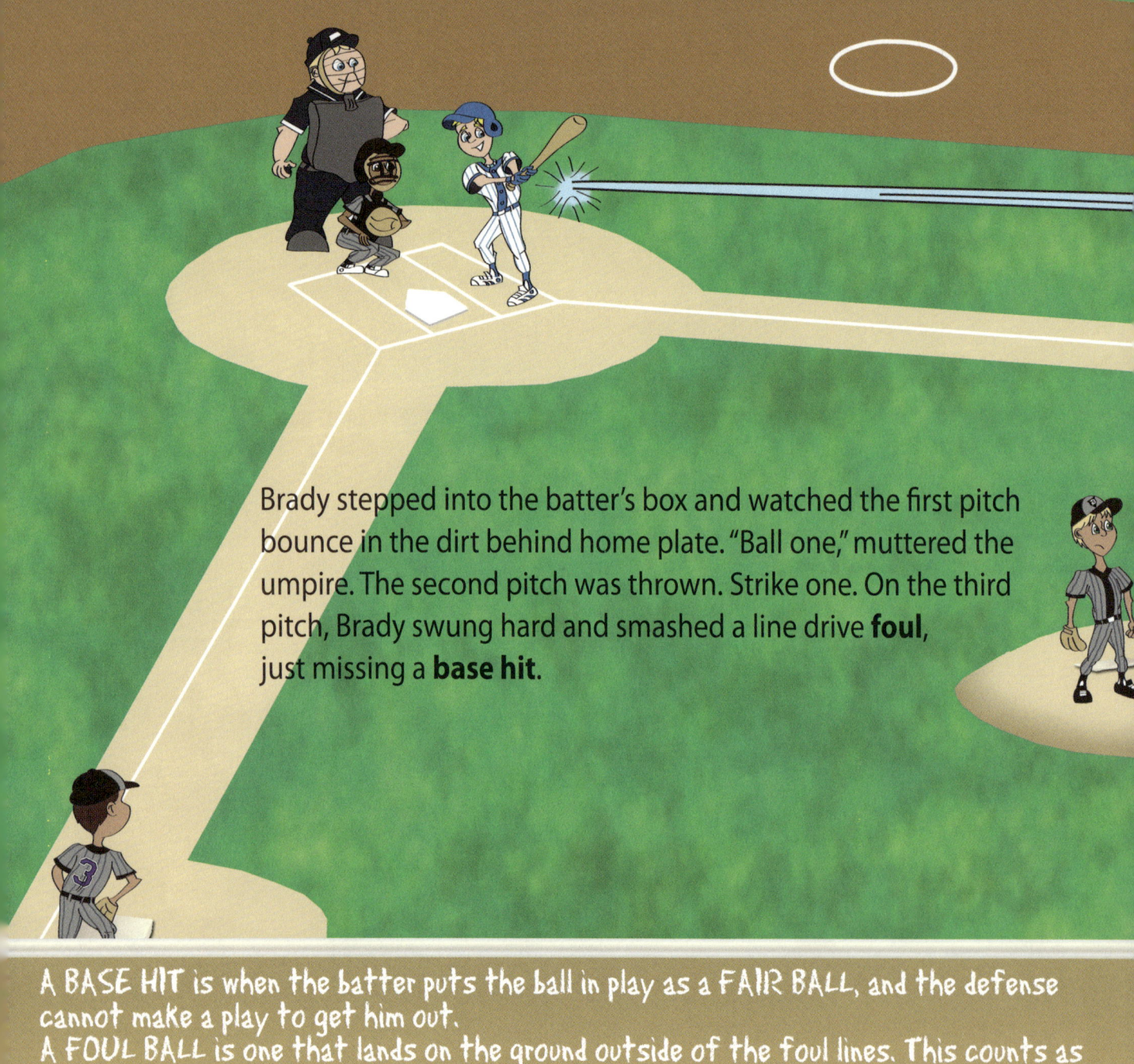

Brady stepped into the batter's box and watched the first pitch bounce in the dirt behind home plate. "Ball one," muttered the umpire. The second pitch was thrown. Strike one. On the third pitch, Brady swung hard and smashed a line drive **foul**, just missing a **base hit**.

A BASE HIT is when the batter puts the ball in play as a FAIR BALL, and the defense cannot make a play to get him out.
A FOUL BALL is one that lands on the ground outside of the foul lines. This counts as a strike on the batter unless he already has two strikes against him. A batter cannot strikeout on a foul ball, but remains with two strikes against him.

Two strikes, thought Brady. *Don't swing for a **home run** – just make good contact.*
Brady stepped up to the plate. The pitch…. SMASH!
Brady roped a **fair ball** down the left field line. He knew he would have at least a **single**, maybe even a **double** or **triple**!

A SINGLE, DOUBLE, TRIPLE, and HOME RUN are the four types of base hits. The name of a base hit reflects how many bases the batter is able to reach before stopping, with a home run meaning the batter came all the way around the bases to score.

Brady watched the left fielder scoop up the ball and set his feet to throw. He put his head down and sprinted around first base. Knowing the throw was coming to second base, Brady made a feet-first **slide** into the base for a double.

A SLIDE is a play in which the base runner attempts to avoid being tagged by sliding into a base. A slide can also help a player to stay on the base after running full speed to get there. A feet-first slide, in which the runner looks to touch the base with his lead foot, is recommended for younger players. A head-first slide can be used by more advanced players by sliding on their stomachs and reaching for the base with their lead hand.

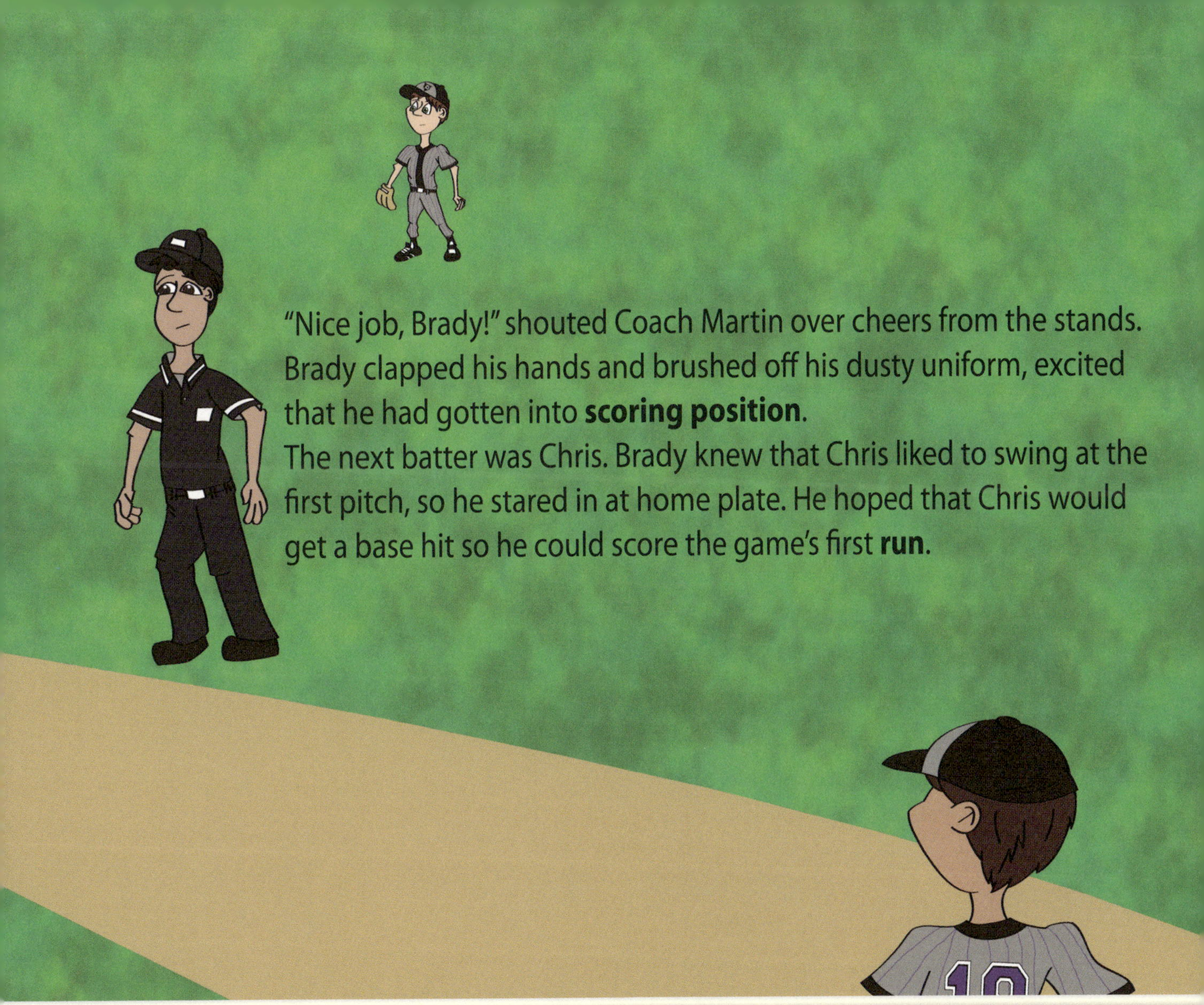

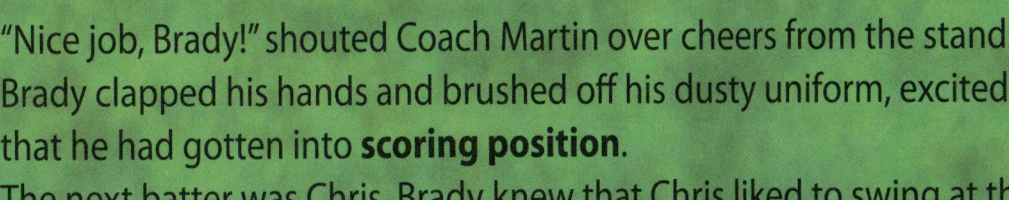

"Nice job, Brady!" shouted Coach Martin over cheers from the stands. Brady clapped his hands and brushed off his dusty uniform, excited that he had gotten into **scoring position**.

The next batter was Chris. Brady knew that Chris liked to swing at the first pitch, so he stared in at home plate. He hoped that Chris would get a base hit so he could score the game's first **run**.

A RUN is the term for a scoring point and happens when a base runner safely touches home plate after circling the bases in order.
SCORING POSITION is the term for when a player reaches second or third base because he may be able to score a run on the next base hit.

POP! Chris belted a single up the middle. With two outs in the inning, Brady shot toward third base on the sound of the bat, watching his **base coach** as he rounded the base. The coach was waving him home! There was going to be a play at the plate. Slide...Tag….

A BASE COACH will typically stand near first and third bases and assist the base runner by telling him either to run through to the next base or to stop. This helps the base runner avoid making outs on the bases.

Safe! Brady scored the game's first run to make it 1-0. He ran to the dugout and was congratulated by his teammates.

Being SAFE on base is the goal of every base runner. Smart base runners will be aware of how the defense is playing the ball and to what base a fielder might be throwing so they can advance safely from base to base.

After making their third out, the Knights ran onto the field as the spectators cheered. Chris grabbed the ball and started taking his warm-up throws. After outs by the first two batters, the third batter stepped in and hit a hard ground ball to James, the Knights' third baseman. James reached down for the ground ball, but it skipped under his glove. The runner was safe at first base on the **error** by James.

James kicked the dirt in frustration.

"You're okay, James," encouraged Brady. "You'll get the next one."

An ERROR is a mistake made by the defense that typically happens when a fielding player fails to catch a ground ball, fly ball, or thrown ball which comes to him. Errors can also occur when a player throws the ball poorly to one of his teammates.

Chris wound up for the next pitch. CRACK!
Oh no, thought Brady as he watched the ball sail over the fence for a home run. The Knights now trailed 2-1.

QUICK TIP: A player who is fielding a ground ball should always attempt to move his feet to get in front of the ball. As the ball comes, he should keep his glove on the ground until the ball is secured. This is called "staying down on a ground ball" and is important for fielding players to perform correctly to avoid making errors.

In the top of the 2nd inning, the Knights came up to bat and had a great start to the inning. Single. Double. Single. Walk. Single. Single. With three more runs on the scoreboard, the Knights led 4-2. Brady was coming up to bat again. A Knight base runner stood at each base.
Bases loaded, nobody out, thought Brady. *Just make contact.*
Brady swatted the first pitch and hit a high fly ball. James was on third base and realized the Dragons' center fielder would make the catch. He decided to **tag up**.

TAGGING UP is when a base runner goes back to his base as the ball is hit in the air. A player who has tagged up on his base can attempt to advance to the next base once the ball is caught – but not before. This play is known as a SACRIFICE FLY. A runner who is off his base when a fly ball is caught can be thrown out if the ball comes back to the base before he does.

When the ball was caught, James broke for home. Here came the throw from the fielder. Brady was wide-eyed in anticipation. Safe! Brady was out, but James had scored a run on the **sacrifice fly**.

QUICK TIP: Instead of tagging up on a fly ball, a runner may decide it's better to go half way to the next base just in case the fielder cannot make the catch. Going half way will help the runner avoid being thrown out on a force out play at the next base if the ball hits the ground.

"Excellent job, boys," said Coach Martin as Brady and James arrived in the dugout. "Yeah, great **base running**!" Brady said with a slap on the back.

BASE RUNNING can be a very important part of the game as the ball is always in play when not being handled by the umpire. The goal of every base runner is to make it to each base safely until ultimately making it home for a run. In order to do this, a good base runner will always know the game situation and understand his role on the bases.

Now with two outs, the Knights still had runners in scoring position. Brady was excited as they led the game 5-2, but he watched as the next two batters struck out swinging.

The top half of the inning was over, so Brady and his teammates sprinted out to the field for defense in the bottom of the 2nd inning.

QUICK TIP: Instead of tagging up on a fly ball, a runner may decide it's better to go half way to the next base just in case the fielder cannot make the catch. Going half way will help the runner avoid being thrown out on a force out play at the next base if the ball hits the ground.

In the bottom of the 2nd, the Dragons led off the inning with several base hits in a row. With another run on the board, the score was now 5-3 Knights. The Dragons had runners at first and second base with nobody out.

Brady chewed his gum nervously. He was hoping for a ground ball so that they could turn a **double play**.

A DOUBLE PLAY happens any time the fielding team makes two outs on a single play, while a TRIPLE PLAY occurs when three outs are made on a play. Double and triple plays can involve strikeouts, fly outs, tag outs, and force outs.

SMACK! The batter hit a soft line drive up the middle, but Brady was in perfect position. He plucked the ball out of the air.
One out, he thought. Then he darted toward second base and stepped on the bag ahead of the base runner trying to get back.
Two outs! The crowd began to buzz.
Brady set his feet to throw to first base for the **triple play**. The runner was scrambling back. The slide… The catch….
"OUT!" thundered the first base umpire over wild cheers from the spectators.
Brady had completed the triple play!

QUICK TIP: The fielding team should typically make an effort to get an out on the lead base runner during the play. However, whenever there are two outs, a team may choose to go for the easiest out in order to complete the inning.

By the end of the 3rd inning, the Dragons had scored three times to take a 6-5 lead. With the Knights batting in the top of the 4th inning, Brady came to the plate with Anthony on first base and his team down by one.

The pitcher hurled the ball toward home plate. Brady made a **check swing** at the ball which was thrown in the dirt.
"Good eye!" yelled Brady's teammates from the dugout.

A CHECK SWING is when a player starts his motion to swing but decides to stop. If the umpire rules that the player did not make a swing attempt, the batter is granted a check swing, and the pitch can be called a ball or a strike depending on its location.

The next pitch was low again. It bounced in the dirt and rolled by the catcher, going all the way to the back-stop for a **wild pitch**. Anthony hustled over to second base. Brady stepped out of the batter's box and adjusted his gloves. Now back in the box, here was the pitch.

Brady took a good swing but barely nicked the top of the ball. It rolled slowly toward the shortstop, so Brady scampered toward first base. The fielder picked up the ball and fired it to first base. Too late! Brady had an infield single.

A WILD PITCH happens when a pitch cannot be caught by the catcher and a base runner advances to his next base as a result. Wild pitches can happen on called balls and strikes, as well as on swinging strikes, as long as the ball is not tipped foul on the swing. On the other hand, an uncaught pitch is considered a *passed ball* if it's simply dropped by the catcher.

Brady's hit had led to a huge moment in the game. With the Knights trailing 6-5, he was the go-ahead run at first base. Brady watched for a **sign** from the third-base coach. Would he tell him to **steal** second base? 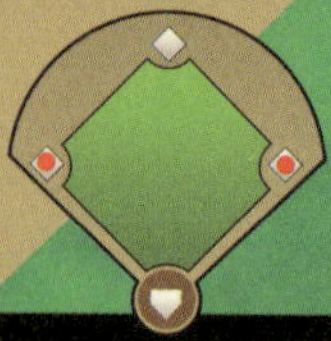
Yes, but he's calling a **hit and run**, Brady thought, reading the hand signals. He took a few steps away from first base for his lead off as the pitcher got set to throw.

The pitcher kicked up his leg. Brady bolted for second base. CRACK! The crowd roared as the ball flew into the left-center field gap. Brady rounded second base. He approached third base. His coach was waving him home!

SIGNS are often used by coaches to secretly communicate with their players on the field. One of the signs used most often is to STEAL a base, which is when base runners try to advance to the next base during the pitch. During a steal, the catcher can receive the pitch and then throw to the base in order to throw out the base stealer.

Brady stepped on third and kept running. Here was the throw. Brady slid wildly into home as a cloud of dust erupted from around the plate. "Safe!" signaled the umpire. Brady scored the go-ahead run, and the Knights were winning 7-6.

In a **HIT AND RUN** play, the offense sends its base runners on a steal and the batter swings at the pitch. The goals of a hit and run play are to make the defense move out of position by having to cover the bases and to have the runners already moving toward their next base when the ball is hit.

Heading into the bottom of the 6th and final inning, the Knights had scored another run and now led 8-6. If they could hold the lead in this inning, they would win the game.

The Dragons' first batter reached base with a single. Brady watched the Dragons' dugout to see if they would send in a **pinch hitter**.

The next batter stepped up to the plate. Here was the pitch.

The batter squared around to **bunt**. But he wasn't bunting for a **sacrifice**; he was trying for a hit!

Brady leapt out of his stance and raced to cover first base as Anthony sprinted toward home plate.

A PINCH HITTER is a substitute batter not currently in the lineup who replaces a player in the batting order. Once used, a pinch hitter will stay in the substituted player's field position for the remainder of the game.

The batter bunted the ball past the pitcher near the first base line. Anthony snatched up the ball with his bare hand. He tossed the ball side-armed to Brady, who got to first base just in time.

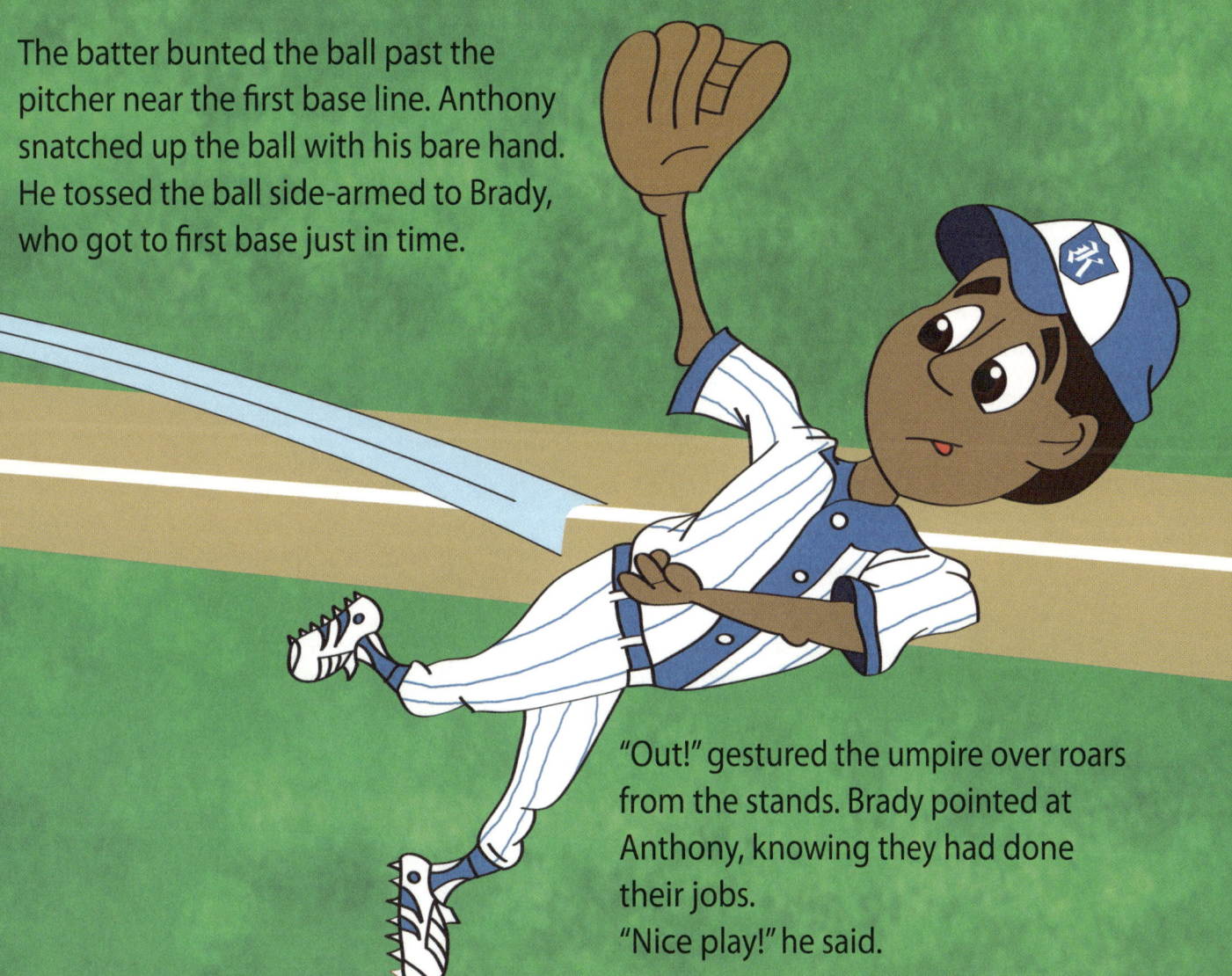

"Out!" gestured the umpire over roars from the stands. Brady pointed at Anthony, knowing they had done their jobs.
"Nice play!" he said.

A BUNT is a play in which the batter doesn't swing, but instead extends the bat across the plate in an effort to gently hit the ball on the ground. A SACRIFICE bunt is used to move base runners up from their current base in exchange for the batter's out. However, a well-placed bunt can also turn into a base hit if the defense cannot make a play on the ball.

The Knights had made a great play for the first out of the inning. The next batter struck out swinging. Now the Knights were only one out away from winning the game. The spectators rose to their feet as the pitcher made his throw.
WHACK! The batter lined the ball over Brady's head and into right field. Brady ran to the outfield grass as the **cut-off man**.

He was looking to hold the tying run at first base, but as the throw came, he missed the catch and the ball fell to the grass.

The CUT-OFF MAN is usually one of the infielders who helps to shorten throws coming from the outfield. On balls hit deep into the outfield, the outfielder will throw the ball to the cut-off man who has run to the shallow outfield to receive the throw. The cut-off man then gets the ball back into the infield to stop the runners from advancing.

34

The batter advanced to second base on Brady's error, and the runner from second scampered home making the score 8-7.
"Now he's in scoring position," Brady grumbled, shaking his head in disgust.

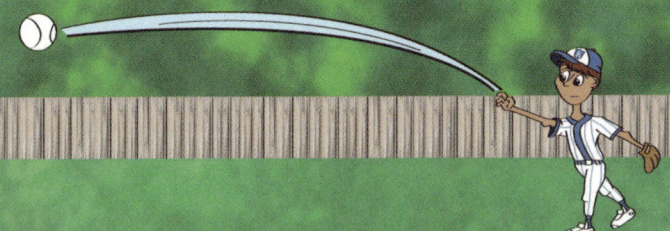

"That's OK, Brady!" shouted Coach Martin from the dugout. "Let's get this out!" Brady got back into position and glared at the next batter, determined to make up for his mistake.

 QUICK TIP: Teams that mishandle the cut-off man throw can allow the offense to take extra bases. The cut-off man's responsibility is to know the game situation and which base runners are most important in that moment.

All eyes in the park were on the field. Chris stepped back onto the mound and took a deep breath. He checked the runner at second base before he wound up to make the pitch.

If this ball is hit anywhere near me, I'm catching it, thought Brady.

POP! A shallow fly ball soared over the infield. Brady sprinted toward right-center field. He knew he was the only player who could get to the ball before it landed.

A base hit would allow the tying run to score. An out would win the game. He had to make the play.
Running full speed, Brady glanced over his shoulder. He was going to have to dive. He leapt.....He stretched....

SMACK! The ball landed squarely in Brady's glove. "OUT!" thundered the umpire as Brady tumbled onto his back, still clutching the ball. His teammates whooped and hollered as they jumped on him in celebration.

Brady had made the final out of the game. The Knights and the Dragons gathered in the infield.
"Great catch, Brady," said the Dragons' players.
Brady's family applauded from the bleachers. He could tell they were proud of him. He was proud too, and he couldn't wait for the next game.

About the Authors:

Gerald Hacker and his wife Amy live in Trussville, Alabama and are the parents of five children. An avid sports fan, Gerald has coached his children's teams in both baseball and basketball. During his years of coaching, Gerald realized the largest obstacle for children entering into youth sports was understanding the rules of the game. This led him to team up with his friend Andrew Wolthers to develop The Rules of the Game series.

Andrew Wolthers enjoyed numerous sports as a youth and played Division I basketball while a student at Northern Arizona University. Andrew coaches youth basketball and soccer throughout the year and currently resides in Hendersonville, Tennessee with his wife Lindsay and their two sons.

Ryan Adamson is an Illustrator and Cartoonist. He lives in Cincinnati, Ohio with his wife Cindy, their cats and dogs. For better or worse, he's a fan of his hometown teams the Cincinnati Bengals and the Reds.